INTRODUCTION

Thank you for using this dictionary, we hope it will help you to learn English prepositions.

This dictionary contains all prepositions, but we'll add more meanings and examples in the next editions until we make the best preposition dictionary in the world (we mean it).

If you found a mistake or you have suggestions,
just email us to learzing@learzing.com

A

ABOARD

Meaning: On or into a ship, aircraft, train, or other vehicle.

Example: I like to read aboard a plane.

Example: She invited 150 people aboard the luxury yacht.

ABOUT

Meaning 1: On the subject of.

Example: I'm reading comics about Superman.

Example: What's she so angry about?

Meaning 2: In many directions in a place.

Example: He wandered about the town for an hour or so.

Example: We looked about the museum for a bit before going on a tour.

Meaning 3: In various parts of a place.

Example: Clothes were lying about the room.

Example: He plays computer games all the time and all the trash is thrown about the room.

ABOVE

Meaning 1: At a higher place or position.

Example: Our plane was flying above the clouds and mountains.

Example: The water came above our knees.

Meaning 2: Of greater importance or of higher quality.

Example: She values her job above her family.

Example: I rate him above most other players of his age.

ACCORDING TO

Meaning: Following, agreeing with or depending on something.

Example: We construct a building and everything goes according to plan.

Example: We should play the game according to the rules.

ACROSS

Meaning: From one side to the other.

Example: There is a bridge across the river.

Example: He walked across the field.

AFTER

Meaning 1: Later than.

Example: I went for a swim after breakfast.

Example: Next day doctor came to check me after the operation.

Meaning 2: Following.

Example: The boy is running after the ball.

Example: Your name comes after mine in the list.

AGAINST

Meaning 1: In opposition to.

Example: Did you vote for or against the candidate?

Example: We're playing against the league champions next week.

Meaning 2: In contact with.

Example: He put his bicycle against the wall.

Example: He leaned his head against the back of his chair.

AHEAD OF

Meaning 1: In front of.

Example: We went to school and Tommy was ahead of us.

Example: He could see that the road ahead of him was clear.

Meaning 2: Earlier than.

Example: I finished the project several days ahead of the deadline.

Example: The election was held six months ahead of schedule.

Meaning 3: Making more progress than someone else.

Example: Sophie is well ahead of the other children in her class.

Example: The Russians were now ahead of them in space research.

ALONG

Meaning 1: From one end to the other.

Example: There are trees along the road.

Example: I looked along the shelves for the book I needed.

Meaning 2: At a particular point on something long.

Example: My office is the second door along the hallway.

Example: Somewhere along this road there's a garage.

ALONG WITH

Meaning: Mentioning additional people or things.

Example: John was arrested along with his wife.

Example: He is learning English along with Hindi.

ALONGSIDE

Meaning: Close to the side of; next to.

Example: The railway runs alongside the road.

Example: The children worked alongside their parents in the field.

AMID (OR AMIDST)

Meaning: Surrounded by; in the middle of.

Example: We camped that day amid a fir forest.

Example: He finished his speech amidst tremendous applause.

AMONG (OR AMONGST)

Meaning: Surrounded by.

Example: She felt lonely among all these strange people.

Example: I found the letter amongst his papers.

ANTI

Meaning: Opposed to; against.

Example: She seems to be anti my idea.

Example: We're very anti smoking in this office.

APART FROM

Meaning: Except for.

Example: Apart from a few scratches, the car was as good as new.

Example: I've finished apart from the last question.

AROUND

Meaning 1: In a circle.

Example: They all sat around the campfire.

Example: He walked around the lake.

Meaning 2: Near, approximately.

Example: Chicken costs around 9 dollars.

Example: There must be around 500 people there.

AS

Meaning: Used to describe the fact that somebody/something has a particular job or function.

Example: She works as a waitress.

Example: You can use that glass as a vase.

AS WELL AS

Meaning: In addition to.

Example: He invited Jack as well as Kate and Peter.

Example: When they go to Austria, they like walking as well as skiing.

ASIDE FROM

Meaning: Except for; besides.

Example: Aside from a mild fever, the boy feels fine.

Example: She has money aside from her possessions.

ASTRIDE

Meaning: With a leg on each side of.

Example: She was sitting astride a horse.

Example: He sat proudly astride his new motorbike.

AT

Meaning 1: Place.

Example: I met her at the hospital.

Example: They're passing through the security check at the airport.

Meaning 2: Time.

Example: We left at 2 o'clock.

Example: I'm busy at the moment - can you call back later?

Meaning 3: Direction.

Example: What are you looking at?

Example: He pointed a gun at her.

Meaning 4: Cause.

Example: They were impatient at the delay.

Example: We were quite excited at the volcano experiment.

Meaning 5: Activity.

Example: I'm good at swimming.

Example: She's hopeless at organizing things.

ATOP

Meaning: On the top of.

Example: The house is situated atop a hill.

Example: Place a scoop of ice cream atop a slice of apple pie.

AWAY FROM

Meaning: Distance.

Example: She had been away from her family for a long time.

Example: I am away from the office until next Tuesday.

B

BAR

Meaning: Except for.

Example: I've read all her books, bar one.

Example: The students all attended, bar two who were ill.

Example: He's the greatest chef of all time bar none. (no one else is better)

BARRING

Meaning: Except if a particular thing happens.

Example: Barring a miracle, he won't walk again.

Example: Barring accidents, we should arrive on time.

BECAUSE OF

Meaning: Reason.

Example: There were so many people in line because of the sale.

Example: He walked slowly because of his bad leg.

BEFORE

Meaning 1: Earlier than.

Example: He arrived before me.

Example: Before leaving he said goodbye to his daughter.

Meaning 2: In front of.

Example: She stood before the passengers and did safety demonstration.

Example: Paula stood before a mirror and brushed out her hair.

Meaning 3: In preference to; with a high priority than.

Example: Yuck! I would rather die before eating this soup!

Example: He worked for the state police for almost 20 years and placed duty before all else.

BEHIND

Meaning 1: At the back of.

Example: Passengers sit in the cab behind the driver.

Example: The sun disappeared behind the clouds.

Meaning 2: Responsible for, the cause of.

Example: He was the man behind the plan to build a new hospital.

Example: What was the reason behind her decision to leave?

BELOW

Meaning 1: At a lower level than.

Example: Below the ground, the subway carries people around the city.

Example: Please do not write below this line.

Meaning 2: Less than a certain number or amount.

Example: They have three children below the age of five.

Example: The college will not accept candidates with test scores below 60.

BENEATH

Meaning: Directly under something or at a lower level.

Example: We took shelter beneath a huge oak tree.

Example: The prisoner dug a tunnel beneath the prison.

BESIDE

Meaning: Next to; by the side of.

Example: He lives in a house beside a small lake.

Example: A young girl offered me a seat and stood beside me.

BESIDES

Meaning: In addition to.

Example: What shall we have besides coffee?

Example: Besides working as a doctor, he also writes novels in his spare time.

BETWEEN

Meaning 1: In the space separating two or more things.

Example: He sat between two women at the airport.

Example: Switzerland lies between France, Germany, Austria and Italy.

Meaning 2: In the period separating two points in time.

Example: The office will be closed between Christmas and New Year.

Example: They often eat fast food between meals.

BEYOND

Meaning 1: Further away than something else.

Example: The road continues beyond the village up into the hills.

Example: We passed the hotel and drove a bit beyond to see the ocean.

Meaning 2: Outside a limit.

Example: He survived the accident, but his car was damaged beyond repair.

Example: Our success was far beyond what we thought possible.

BUT

Meaning: Except; apart from.

Example: All but one person left the movie theater.

Example: We've had nothing but trouble with this car.

BY

Meaning 1: Near, at the side of.

Example: Jenny is sitting by the window.

Example: Come and sit by me.

Meaning 2: Cause.

Example: I was frightened by the noise.

Example: I took her umbrella by mistake.

Meaning 3: Method.

Example: I learned English by listening to audio lessons.

Example: They thought about flying to Boston but decided to go by car.

Meaning 4: According to.

Example: By my watch, it's two o'clock.

Example: I could tell by the look on her face that something terrible had happened.

Meaning 5: Not later than.

Example: I'll have it done by tomorrow.

Example: Can you finish the work by five o'clock?

Meaning 6: Measurements or amounts.

Example: Their wages were increased by 15 percent.

Example: Freelance workers are paid by the hour.

Example: We rented the car by the day.

BY MEANS OF

Meaning: Through.

Example: You open a door by means of its handle.

Example: The teacher explained the exercise by means of an example.

C

CIRCA

Meaning: About, approximately (used before a date).

Example: The church was built circa 1860.

Example: The Greek philosopher Diogenes was born circa 412 BC.

CONCERNING

Meaning: About.

Example: The teacher will talk to me concerning my son's behavior.

Example: He asked several questions concerning the future of the company.

CONSIDERING

Meaning: Taking into account; in view of.

Example: He ran very well considering his age.

Example: Considering her lack of experience, it is surprising she has achieved so much.

COUNTING

Meaning: Including.

Example: There are six of us in the family, or seven counting my dog.

Example: That makes $70, not counting the tax.

D

DESPITE

Meaning: Without being affected by; in spite of.

Example: He went swimming despite the cold water.

Example: Despite applying for hundreds of jobs, he is still out of work.

DOWN

Meaning: From higher to lower.

Example: The stone rolled down the hill.

Example: She's walking down the steps.

DUE TO

Meaning: Because of.

Example: The company's financial losses were due to poor management.

Example: Evening classes were cancelled due to heavy snow.

DURING

Meaning 1: Through a period of time.

Example: During the summer season, all the hotels are full.

Example: Many creatures stay underground during daylight hours.

Meaning 2: At one point within a period of time.

Example: They fell asleep during the meeting.

Example: He was taken to the hospital during the night.

E

EXCEPT

Meaning: Not including, other than.

Example: The office works every day except Sunday.

Example: This door should remain locked except in an emergency.

F

FOLLOWING

Meaning: After or as a result of a particular event.

Example: Following the dinner, there will be a dance.

Example: He couldn't work following his illness.

Example: He took charge of the family business following his father's death.

FOR

Meaning 1: Intended for.

Example: This gift is for you!

Example: I bought some flowers for Chloe.

Meaning 2: Purpose.

Example: He put all his dirty clothes in a pile for washing.

Example: I'm sorry, the books are not for sale.

Meaning 3: Because of.

Example: He spent 15 years in prison for murder.

Example: Scotland is famous for its spectacular countryside.

Meaning 4: Time or distance.

Example: The desert stretched for hundreds of miles in all directions.

Example: She's out of the office for a few days next week.

Meaning 5: Considering.

Example: My grandmother is pretty active for her age.

Example: He's not bad for a beginner.

Meaning 6: Representing.

Example: He plays for Manchester United.

Example: I'm speaking for all of us when I say how sorry we are.

Meaning 7: In order to get or have.

Example: I'm late, I have to wait 15 minutes for the next train.

Example: I've applied for several jobs since leaving university.

FROM

Meaning 1: Source or origin.

Example: She got a letter from her friend.

Example: He keeps in touch with his friends from college.

Meaning 2: Time.

Example: Drinks will be served from seven o'clock.

Example: The oldest part of the castle dates from the 13th century.

Meaning 3: Distance.

Example: It's about two kilometers from the airport to our hotel.

Example: My office is about a mile from here.

Meaning 4: Material.

Example: Steel is made from iron.

Example: All her jars are made from clay.

Meaning 5: Cause.

Example: The number of deaths from road accidents continues to rise.

Example: She made her money from investing in property.

Meaning 6: Change.

Example: The story was translated from Turkish to English.

Example: She went from being an ordinary looking woman to being a great sex symbol.

Meaning 7: Considering.

Example: Just from looking at the clouds, I would say it's going to rain.

Example: It's difficult to guess what they will conclude from the evidence.

FURTHER TO

Meaning: Used in letters, emails, etc. to refer to a previous letter, email, conversation, etc.

Example: Further to your email, I have spoken to Mr. Brown.

Example: Further to our conversation of last Friday, I would like to book the conference centre for June 26.

G

GIVEN

Meaning: Taking into account; considering.

Example: Given his age, he's remarkably active.

Example: Given her interest in children, teaching seems the right job for her.

GONE

Meaning: Later or older than.

Example: I said I'd be home by six and it's already gone seven.

Example: He's gone 50. He must be nearly 60 years old.

I

IN

Meaning 1: Inside.

Example: Monkeys live in the jungle.

Example: Is Mark still in bed?

Meaning 2: During.

Example: Let's meet again in the morning, at around 9.30.

Example: The first robots were invented in the 1920s.

Meaning 3: Distance.

Example: It's about two kilometers from the airport to our hotel.

Example: My office is about a mile from here.

Meaning 4: Material.

Example: Steel is made from iron.

Example: All her jars are made from clay.

Meaning 5: Cause.

Example: The number of deaths from road accidents continues to rise.

Example: She made her money from investing in property.

Meaning 6: Change.

Example: The story was translated from Turkish to English.

Example: She went from being an ordinary looking woman to being a great sex symbol.

Meaning 7: Considering.

Example: Just from looking at the clouds, I would say it's going to rain.

Example: It's difficult to guess what they will conclude from the evidence.

IN ADDITION TO

Meaning: Besides; as well as.

Example: He ordered a salad in addition to the pizza.

Example: In addition to me, there were two people in the line.

IN BETWEEN

Meaning: In the space that separates two things.

Example: I go to the gym on Mondays, on Saturdays, and sometimes in between.

Example: He is in between the two opinions. He wants to compromise.

IN CASE OF

Meaning: If and when something happens.

Example: In case of fire, go immediately to the nearest emergency exit.

Example: Call me in case of any emergency.

IN FAVOR OF

Meaning 1: In support of; supporting.

Example: We are in favor of his promotion to president.

Example: Many people are in favor of the death penalty.

Meaning 1: Preferring to choose something that you believe is better.

Example: We canceled our vacation in favor of buying a new car.

Example: He left school after just three years in favor of a professional sports career.

IN FRONT OF

Meaning: Close to the front part of something.

Example: My car's parked in front of your house.

Example: She made a selfie in front of the mirror.

IN SPITE OF

Meaning: Even though; not stopped by; regardless of.

Example: I went swimming in spite of the cold water.

Example: He was very fast in spite of being terribly overweight.

IN VIEW OF

Meaning: Because of; considering.

Example: In view of the high cost of gasoline, I sold my car.

Example: In view of the shortage of time, each person may only speak for five minutes.

INSIDE

Meaning 1: On the inner part of.

Example: What's inside the box?

Example: Go inside the house.

Meaning 2: In less than.

Example: The new faster trains can do the journey inside two hours.

Example: He swam the 200 meters just inside the European record.

INSTEAD OF

Meaning: In place of; as an alternative to something.

Example: You can have rice instead of potatoes.

Example: You can use milk instead of cream in this recipe.

INTO

Meaning 1: Inside.

Example: He put his hands into his pockets.

Example: She dived into the water.

Meaning 2: In the direction of.

Example: She was looking straight into his eyes.

Example: Please speak clearly into the microphone.

Meaning 3: Change in state.

Example: Can you translate this passage into German?

Example: The fruit can be made into jam.

L

LESS

Meaning: Minus.

Example: He earns $500 a week, less tax.

Example: The total is 30 dollars, less the five dollars deposit that you paid.

LIKE

Meaning 1: Similar to.

Example: He's very like his father.

Example: She's wearing a dress like mine.

Meaning 2: As if.

Example: It looks like rain.

Example: He sounded like he'd only just woken up.

M

MINUS

Meaning 1: Subtract.

Example: Seven minus three equals four.

Example: We earned 600 dollars minus travel expenses.

Meaning 2: Without.

Example: He left the restaurant minus his hat.

Example: We're going to be minus a car for a while.

N

NEAR

Meaning 1: Not far away in distance.

Example: Do you live near here?

Example: Jack likes to sit near a window on a plane.

Meaning 2: Not far away in time.

Example: She's near the age of 70.

Example: It's December 23rd - we are very near Christmas Day.

Meaning 3: Close to a particular state.

Example: She was near to tears.

Example: He looked near exhaustion.

NEXT TO

Meaning: Very near; beside.

Example: I am sitting next to my father.

Example: She's going to sleep next to her baby.

NOTWITHSTANDING

Meaning: Without being affected by; despite.

Example: He went for a walk, notwithstanding the rain.

Example: Notwithstanding a brilliant defense, he was found guilty.

O

O F

Meaning 1: Containing or consisting of.

Example: Can I have a cup of coffee?

Example: He wrote a book of short stories.

Meaning 2: Possession, belonging, or origin.

Example: One of my friends is a good chess player.

Example: The color of his tie matches his suit.

Meaning 3: Amount.

Example: There were hundreds of people on the streets.

Example: She broke the world record by a tenth of a second.

Meaning 4: Position.

Example: I left the book on top of my desk.

Example: He lives in the center of London.

Meaning 5: Typical or characteristic of.

Example: She has the face of an angel.

Example: She plays the piano with the skill of a professional.

Meaning 6: Used to describe a particular day.

Example: Today is the eleventh of July.

Example: April Fools' Day is celebrated on the first of April.

Meaning 7: Made or consisting of; having.

Example: The barman made a cocktail of vodka and orange juice.

Example: A feeling of great sadness came over him.

Meaning 8: Judgement.

Example: He was a man of great charm.

Example: It was rude of her to laugh at him.

Meaning 9: Relating to; about.

Example: Speaking of Elizabeth, here she is.

Example: She bought a map of the area so that she wouldn't get lost.

Meaning 10: Caused by.

Example: He died of a heart attack.

Example: She is frightened of spiders.

Meaning 11: Comparing.

Example: He's the oldest of three brothers.

Example: The Eiffel Tower is the most famous of the monuments in Paris.

Meaning 12: Showing distance from something in place or time.

Example: We live within a mile of the school.

Example: She came within two seconds of beating the world record.

Meaning 13: During.

Example: My grandpa likes to relax with a pipe of an evening.

Example: We would often have a walk of a morning until 12 o'clock.

OFF

Meaning 1: Down or away from.

Example: The cup fell off the table and broke.

Example: She got off the bus at the next stop.

Meaning 2: Close to.

Example: The restaurant is just off the main road.

Example: You'll find a bathroom just off the master bedroom.

Meaning 3: Away from work or duty.

Example: He's had ten days off school.

Example: I had 6 months off when my son was born.

O N

Meaning 1: Above.

Example: Please don't put your shoes on the table.

Example: Ow, you're standing on my foot!

Meaning 2: Connected.

Example: Dogs should be kept on leashes in public.

Example: We could hang this picture on the wall next to the door.

Meaning 3: A day or date.

Example: What are you doing on Friday?

Example: My birthday is on January 7th.

Meaning 4: Written, printed, or drawn.

Example: Do you recognize the writing on the envelope?

Example: His initials were engraved on the back of his watch.

Meaning 5: Transport.

Example: I love traveling on trains.

Example: He was on the plane from New York.

Meaning 6: A condition or process.

Example: He accidentally set his bed on fire.

Example: Max is on vacation this week.

Meaning 7: Recorded or performed.

Example: He's writing a new book on his old typewriter.

Example: I wish there was more jazz on the radio.

Meaning 8: Cause of pain or injury.

Example: She burned her finger on the candle.

Example: He smashed his elbow on the door.

Meaning 9: Relating to.

Example: I've got nothing to say on the matter.

Example: He gave me a book on gardening for my birthday.

Meaning 10: Money.

Example: He spent €180 on a hat.

Example: I've wasted a lot of money on this car.

Meaning 11: Next to or along the side of.

Example: A new coffee shop opened on the main street.

Example: Strasbourg is on the border of France and Germany.

Meaning 12: Member.

Example: There are no women on the committee.

Example: How many people are on your staff?

Meaning 13: Tool.

Example: We spoke on the phone.

Example: Chris is on drums and Mike's on bass guitar.

Meaning 14: Again.

Example: The government suffered defeat on defeat in the local elections.

Example: Wave on wave of refugees has crossed the border to escape the war.

Meaning 15: Comparison.

Example: Sales are up on last year.

Example: Subscriptions are down by 66,000 on last year and that is a serious situation.

Meaning 16: Having an effect.

Example: He's hard on his kids.

Example: Marty is always playing jokes on people.

Meaning 17: Possessing.

Example: Do you have any money on you?

Example: I don't have my driver's license on me.

ON ACCOUNT OF

Meaning: Because of.

Example: She had to quit her job on account of her pregnancy.

Example: The camping trip ended early on account of the rain.

ON TOP OF

Meaning: On the highest point or uppermost surface of.

Example: There was a pile of books on top of the table.

Example: There's a cross on top of the church.

ONTO

Meaning 1: Movement.

Example: Move the books onto the second shelf.

Example: He climbed onto the roof to get a better view.

Meaning 2: Direction.

Example: The window looked out onto the terrace.

Example: The building faced onto the main road.

Meaning 3: Adding.

Example: Somehow his name had got onto the list of candidates.

Example: To form the plural, just add 's' or 'es' onto the end.

OPPOSITE

Meaning: Across from or facing someone or something.

Example: I sat opposite him during the meal.

Example: The bank is opposite the supermarket.

OTHER THAN

Meaning: Except for; besides.

Example: He owns nothing other than his suit.

Example: Other than one sister, she has no close relatives.

OUT OF

Meaning 1: No longer in.

Example: The patient is now out of danger.

Example: I really had to drag myself out of bed this morning.

Meaning 2: Made of.

Example: The dress was made out of silk.

Example: He carves toys out of wood and sells them.

Meaning 3: Because of.

Example: I took the job out of necessity because we had no money left.

Example: Just out of interest, how old is your wife?

Meaning 4: From among.

Example: Out of all my friends, she is the most ambitious.

Example: Nine out of ten people said they liked the product.

Meaning 5: Origin.

Example: I paid for the laptop out of my savings.

Example: She dresses like a character out of a 19th-century novel.

OUTSIDE

Meaning: Situated or moving out of somewhere.

Example: He was sitting at a table outside the café.

Example: You can park your car outside our house.

OUTSIDE OF

Meaning: Except for.

Example: Outside of us three, no one knows anything about this secret.

Example: There was nothing they could do, outside of hoping things would get better.

OVER

Meaning 1: Above.

Example: He held the umbrella over both of us.

Example: The horse jumped over the fence.

Meaning 2: Covering.

Example: He put a blanket over my shoulders.

Example: She put her hand over her mouth to stop herself from screaming.

Meaning 3: Across from one side to the other.

Example: She is always chatting with her neighbor over the garden fence.

Example: She rubbed sun lotion over her entire body.

Meaning 4: Falling.

Example: He tripped over a banana peel lying on the floor.

Example: The coin rolled over the edge of the table.

Meaning 5: About.

Example: There's no point in arguing over something so unimportant.

Example: There are worries over the future of the steel industry.

Meaning 6: During.

Example: Can we discuss this over lunch?

Example: She made a lot of changes over the past six months.

Meaning 7: Feeling better.

Example: It takes you a while to get over an illness like that.

Example: His girlfriend broke up with him last year and he's not over her yet.

Meaning 8: Control.

Example: He ruled over a great empire.

Example: A good teacher has an easy authority over a class.

Meaning 9: Using; by means of.

Example: They spoke over the phone.

Example: We heard the news over the radio.

P

PAST

Meaning 1: In or to a position that is further than a particular point.

Example: She walked right past me without noticing me.

Example: Back in the 1960s he had hair down past his shoulders.

Meaning 2: After a particular time.

Example: It's ten minutes past three.

Example: It was past midnight when we got home.

Meaning 3: Above or further than a particular point or stage.

Example: She's past the age where she needs a babysitter.

Example: Unemployment is now past the 3 million mark.

PENDING

Meaning: While waiting for something to happen.

Example: Sales of the drug have been stopped, pending further research.

Example: They are being held in jail pending trial.

PER

Meaning: For each; for every.

Example: The speed limit is 80 miles per hour.

Example: Rooms cost $50 per person, per night.

PLUS

Meaning 1: Used when adding something.

Example: One plus three is four.

Example: Membership is 350 dollars per year plus tax.

Meaning 2: And also.

Example: There will be four adults traveling, plus two children.

Example: We'll need a washing machine and cooker, plus a new bed.

PRO

Meaning: Supporting or agreeing with something.

Example: She's really pro gay rights.

Example: Are you pro smoking, despite the risks?

R

REGARDING

Meaning: About.

Example: I have a question regarding your last statement.

Example: Call me if you have any problems regarding your work.

REGARDLESS OF

Meaning: Without being affected or influenced by.

Example: We run every morning, regardless of the weather.

Example: The club welcomes all new members regardless of age.

RESPECTING

Meaning: Concerning; regarding.

Example: He began to have serious worries respecting his car.

Example: Respecting your earlier question, I'd like to make an additional comment.

R O U N D

Meaning 1: Around; in a circular direction or position.

Example: The Earth goes round the Sun.

Example: She wears a gold cross round her neck.

Meaning 2: In various parts of a place.

Example: We traveled round the country.

Example: There's a virus going round the school.

Meaning 3: Surrounding.

Example: They all sat round the table.

Example: There was a high brick wall round the garden.

Meaning 4: In a particular direction.

Example: I live round the corner.

Example: There are two entrances - one at the front and one round the back.

S

SAVE

Meaning: Except; other than.

Example: He found all the lost documents save one.

Example: They knew nothing about her save her name.

SAVE FOR

Meaning: Except for; but.

Example: Everyone came to the office party, save for Bob who had to work.

Example: I am available on weekdays, save for Thursdays.

SINCE

Meaning: From a time in the past until a later time.

Example: He has lived in the United States since 2005.

Example: I've known Jane since she was born.

T

THAN

Meaning 1: Used to join two parts of a comparison.

Example: I'm older than her.

Example: He loves me more than you do.

Meaning 2: Used for comparing amounts, numbers, distances, etc.

Example: He's a famous writer. He wrote more than 20 books.

Example: It's less than a mile to the beach.

THANKS TO

Meaning: Because of; with the help of.

Example: Thanks to the treatment, your condition has improved.

Example: Thanks to the heavy curtains on my windows, I'm able to sleep even when the sun's shining.

THROUGH

Meaning 1: From one side or end to the other

Example: We drove through the tunnel.

Example: The bullet went straight through him.

Meaning 2: From the beginning to the end of a period of time.

Example: I lost interest half way through the football match.

Example: The children are too young to sit through a concert.

Meaning 3: As a result of.

Example: The error occurred through my own stupidity.

Example: You can only achieve success through hard work.

Meaning 4: Using.

Example: She met her husband through a dating website.

Example: Public schools are financed through taxes.

THROUGHOUT

Meaning 1: In every part of.

Example: Pollution is a serious problem in major cities throughout the world.

Example: The company has stores throughout the United States and Canada.

Meaning 2: During the whole period of time.

Example: The museum is open daily throughout the year.

Example: She's had many different positions throughout her career.

TILL

Meaning: Up to; until.

Example: You'll have to wait till tomorrow.

Example: The supermarket is open till midnight.

TO

Meaning 1: (Infinitive).

Example: She agreed to help.

Example: I don't know what to do.

Meaning 2: In the direction of.

Example: We're going to town on the bus.

Example: We went to Prague last year.

Meaning 3: Receiving.

Example: He gave that book to his sister.

Example: I am deeply grateful to my parents.

Meaning 4: Until.

Example: It's only two weeks to Christmas.

Example: He drank himself to death.

Meaning 5: Connection.

Example: The paper was stuck to the wall with tape.

Example: Attach this rope to the front of the car.

Meaning 6: Against.

Example: The children stood back to back to see who was tallest.

Example: They stood face to face, staring at each other.

Meaning 7: Matching or belonging to.

Example: My dad gave me the keys to his car.

Example: I gave her the password to my computer..

Meaning 8: In honor or memory of.

Example: The book is dedicated to her son.

Example: I proposed a toast to the bride and the groom.

Meaning 9: For each.

Example: There are three children to each teacher.

Example: This car does about 40 miles to the gallon.

Meaning 10: Between.

Example: There were probably 30 to 35 people there.

Example: We have allowed two to four drinks per person.

Meaning 11: At the same time as music or other sound.

Example: I like exercising to music.

Example: I awoke to the sound of birds singing.

Meaning 12: Attitude or reaction.

Example: To her surprise, she saw that he was crying.

Example: His music isn't really to my taste.

Meaning 13: Compared with.

Example: Paul beat me by three games to two.

Example: She was old enough to be his mother - he looked about thirty to her sixty.

TOUCHING

Meaning: On the subject of; concerning.

Example: Touching the issue of education, English should be taught in all schools.

Example: Touching the subject of our conversation, would you please forward me all the relevant documentation?

TOWARD/TOWARDS

Meaning 1: In the direction of.

Example: She stood up and walked toward him.

Example: The hurricane is heading toward Florida.

Meaning 2: In relation to.

Example: He was warm and tender towards her.

Example: My father feels really bitter toward my boyfriend.

Meaning 3: Near to.

Example: Our seats were toward the back of the theater.

Example: I'll phone you some time towards the end of the week.

Meaning 4: For the purpose of.

Example: I'm saving up to buy a car, and dad gave me some money toward it.

Example: Government should be working toward a cleaner environment.

U

UNDER

Meaning 1: Lower position.

Example: She put the thermometer under my tongue.

Example: Have you looked under the bed?

Meaning 2: Less than.

Example: She ran her first marathon in under three hours.

Example: The total cost of the project is just under $2 million.

Meaning 3: Control.

Example: The company became the biggest in the country under his firm leadership.

Example: He's a colonel, with hundreds of soldiers under him.

UNDERNEATH

Meaning: Under; below.

Example: The tunnel goes right underneath the city.

Example: This jacket's too big, even with a sweater underneath.

UNLIKE

Meaning 1: Different from.

Example: Dan is actually very nice, unlike his brother.

Example: Her last book is unlike anything else she has written.

Meaning 2: Not typical.

Example: It's unlike you to be quiet - is something wrong?

Example: Jackie must be worried about something, it's unlike her to be so tense.

UNTIL

Meaning: Up to a particular time or event.

Example: He continued to get a salary until the end of March.

Example: She waited until her coffee had cooled down before taking a sip.

UP

Meaning 1: To or in a higher position.

Example: I followed him up the stairs.

Example: The spider crept up the wall.

Meaning 2: At the top of.

Example: We had to rescue our cat from up the tree.

Example: Her office is up those steps to your right.

Meaning 3: Along.

Example: She walked up the street, reading messages on her phone.

Example: Up the river, in the distance, was the rescue boat.

UPON

Meaning: On.

Example: Upon her head she wore a black velvet hat.

Example: He insisted upon knowing the truth.

UP TO

Meaning: Moving near to.

Example: I'm too shy to go up to them and say hello.

Example: Two women ran up to us, shouting in Spanish.

V

VERSUS

Meaning: Against.

Example: In this match white team is playing against red team.

Example: We are waiting for a court decision in the case of Smith versus Watts.

VIA

Meaning 1: By means of.

Example: I have sent the file via email.

Example: I only found out about it via my sister.

Meaning 2: Through a place.

Example: We flew from London to Moscow via Berlin.

Example: The plan was to carry gas via Iran to Turkey.

W

WITH

Meaning 1: Together.

Example: She lives with her parents.

Example: I think I'll have some ice cream with my pie.

Meaning 2: Using something.

Example: I made this table with my own hands.

Example: He was shot at close range with a pistol.

Meaning 3: Having.

Example: He's married with three children.

Example: She's been in bed all week with flu.

Meaning 4: Concerning.

Example: Be careful with the glasses.

Example: Are you pleased with the result?

Meaning 5: Containing or covering.

Example: My playroom is full with toys.

Example: Sprinkle the dish with salt.

Meaning 6: Because of; as a result of.

Example: I was trembling with fear.

Example: His fingers were numb with cold.

Meaning 7: In opposition to; against.

Example: I've been arguing with my wife all morning.

Example: It's difficult for a small supermarket to compete with the big supermarkets.

Meaning 8: Separation.

Example: I'd rather not part with my cash.

Example: She's just broken up with her boyfriend.

Meaning 9: Comparison.

Example: I have nothing in common with my sister.

Example: This road is quite busy compared with ours.

Meaning 10: Changing as time passes.

Example: This wine will improve with years.

Example: The risk of developing cancer increases with age.

Meaning 11: Despite.

Example: With all her faults I still love her.

Example: With all our differences, we are still good friends.

Meaning 12: A wish or instruction.

Example: Away with you! (= Go away!)

Example: On with the show! (= Let it continue.)

WITH REGARD TO

Meaning: Concerning; about.

Example: With regard to your invoice, it will be paid as soon as possible.

Example: I am writing to you with regard to your son's behavior in class.

WITHIN

Meaning 1: Inside a period of time.

Example: Can you complete the work within a month?

Example: You should receive a reply within seven days.

Meaning 2: Inside an area.

Example: The ticket gives students unlimited free travel within the UK.

Example: The target was now within range and so he took aim and fired.

WITHOUT

Meaning: In the absence of.

Example: I left without my umbrella.

Example: I can't see without my glasses.